Iroquois

F.A. BIRD

CONTENT CONSULTANT: GERALD F. REID, PHD

Checkerboard Library

An Imprint of Abdo Publishing
abdobooks.com

ABDOBOOKS.COM

Published by Abdo Publishing, a division of ABDO, PO Box 398166, Minneapolis, Minnesota 55439.
Copyright © 2022 by Abdo Consulting Group, Inc. International copyrights reserved in all countries.
No part of this book may be reproduced in any form without written permission from the publisher.
Checkerboard Library™ is a trademark and logo of Abdo Publishing.

Printed in the United States of America, North Mankato, Minnesota
102021
012022

THIS BOOK CONTAINS
RECYCLED MATERIALS

Design and Production: Mighty Media, Inc.
Editor: Liz Salzmann
Cover Photograph: Avalon.red/Alamy Photo
Interior Photographs: Ad_hominem/Shutterstock Images, p. 7; Alina Zienowicz/Wikimedia Commons,
    p. 13; Bob Hilscher/Shutterstock Images, p. 29; Brian Lasenby/Shutterstock Images, p. 23; Courtesy
    of the Iroquois Indian Museum, pp. 17, 19; Dennis W Donohue/Shutterstock Images, p. 27; German
    Vizulis/Shutterstock Images, p. 25; hiramtom/iStockphoto, p. 21; igorsm8/Shutterstock Images, p. 11;
    Library and Archives Canada/Flickr, p. 15; scgerding/iStockphoto, p. 5; SkyF/iStockphoto, p. 9

Library of Congress Control Number: 2021943036

Publisher's Cataloging-in-Publication Data
Names: Bird, F.A., author.
Title: Iroquois / by F.A. Bird
Description: Minneapolis, Minnesota : Abdo Publishing, 2022 | Series: Native American nations | Includes
    online resources and index.
Identifiers: ISBN 9781532197192 (lib. bdg.) | ISBN 9781098219321 (ebook)
Subjects: LCSH: Iroquois Indians--Juvenile literature. | Indians of North America--Juvenile literature. |
    Indigenous peoples--Social life and customs--Juvenile literature. | Cultural anthropology--Juvenile
    literature.
Classification: DDC 973.0497--dc23

Contents

CHAPTER 1

Homelands

The Iroquois are also known as the Haudenosaunee (ho-dee-no-sho-nee). It is their preferred name for their people. The original Iroquois homelands covered parts of present-day Ohio, Pennsylvania, New York, Quebec, and Ontario.

Forests covered Iroquois land. The woods were home to deer, bear, turkey, rabbit, squirrel, beaver, and porcupine. Many streams and rivers flowed into the lakes, especially Lake Ontario. These waters contained trout, pike, perch, bass, salmon, turtles, and eels. Swans, geese, and ducks swam in the lakes.

Today, the Iroquois live in New York, Wisconsin, Oklahoma, Quebec, and Ontario. In addition, there are many thousands of Iroquois living in cities and towns across the United States and Canada.

The Iroquois homelands include Lake Ontario. It is one of the Great Lakes.

CHAPTER 2

Society

The original five Iroquois nations were the Mohawk, Oneida, Onondaga, Cayuga, and Seneca. They joined together to form the Haudenosaunee. It means "People of the Longhouse." The English called this **alliance** the Five Nations of the Iroquois **Confederacy**.

In 1722, relatives of these nations left North Carolina. They were called the Tuscarora. The Tuscarora traveled to New York and joined the Haudenosaunee. The Five Nations became Six Nations.

Today, 50 chiefs and 49 **clan** mothers lead the Haudenosaunee. This Grand Council makes important decisions for the Confederacy and its individual nations.

THE IROQUOIS HOMELANDS

CHAPTER 3

Homes

A longhouse was a common type of Iroquois home. The women of an entire **clan**, their husbands, and their children could live in one longhouse. A longhouse frame was made of wooden posts. The frame was covered with sheets of elm bark. Strips of bark were carefully cut and pressed flat with rocks.

Inside the longhouse, each family had its own living area. Each living area had a cooking pit with a **smoke hole** in the ceiling.

The Iroquois slept on platforms. In the poles above their platforms, they hung and stored items like corn. Under the platforms, they stored dried beans and squash in big clay pots.

An Iroquois longhouse

CHAPTER 4

Food

The Iroquois farmed, hunted, and fished. They also gathered food that grew naturally, such as wild roots, berries, plums, cherries, and nuts. Each spring, women planted corn, beans, and squash in fields around the village. The crops were harvested in September or October.

Iroquois men hunted all year. They shot deer with bows and arrows. They trapped bear, beaver, rabbits, ducks, and geese. Iroquois families traveled to streams and lakes to catch fish. They made fishing lines and nets from twisted plant fibers. They made hooks from bird and fish bones. The Iroquois dried most of the fish they caught. They hung them in the **rafters** above the longhouse platforms.

Corn, beans, and squash are known as the "Three Sisters." That's because they grow from Mother Earth.

CHAPTER 5

Clothing

The Iroquois made clothing from animal furs and elk and deer hides. Women wore deerskin dresses, shirts, and skirts. They decorated their clothing with porcupine **quills**. After contact with Europeans, Iroquois women also used glass beads.

Men wore leather **breechcloths**. They hung down in the front and back. Both men and women wore leggings and moccasins. Men and women also had winter robes of bear, buffalo, or elk hides.

Iroquois men wore a hat called a *gustoweh*. It was made from curved wood splints and covered with feathers. The number of eagle feathers on the top of the hat told which Iroquois nation the man was from. Today, Iroquois people usually only wear the traditional style of clothing on special occasions.

A *gustoweh* on display at the National Museum of the American Indian in Washington, DC

CHAPTER 6

Crafts

The Iroquois wove cornhusks together to make rugs, sleeping mats, sandals, and dolls for children. The Iroquois used **wampum** beads to record history and for trade. The Iroquois got seashells needed to make wampum beads from **Indigenous** people who lived near the ocean.

Wampum beads are strung on strings. Each Iroquois Nation is represented by different combinations of bead colors. Wampum beads are also woven into belts that tell Iroquois history.

One type of wampum belt is known as the "Two-Row Wampum." It has two rows of purple beads. One row stands for the white man's laws and customs. The other stands for the Iroquois laws and customs. This shows that there are two sets of laws and customs. It also shows that neither group should interfere with the other's laws or customs.

Six Nations Iroquois chiefs reading wampum belts

CHAPTER 7

Family

Iroquois men and women had to marry someone from a different **clan**. The mothers of a couple who wanted to get married had to agree that the marriage was good. If the mothers did not agree, then the couple could not be married. After marriage, the couple would live in the woman's family's longhouse.

Girls learned from their mothers and other female relatives how to sew, gather food, and plant crops. Young girls also learned by playing with cornhusk dolls. And they learned by watching nature.

Fathers taught their sons how to make arrowheads. They showed them how to hunt, fish, and trade. They also taught them how to defend themselves.

All children learned the traditional songs and dances. And they learned how to use plants to make medicine.

Some cornhusk dolls had faces made from dried apples.

CHAPTER 8

Children

An Iroquois baby was bundled up and gently tied to a cradleboard. The mother carried the cradleboard on her back. Or she could lean it against a tree next to her as she worked.

Cradleboards had a protective wooden band in front of the baby's head. If the cradleboard fell, the band would protect the baby from injury. Iroquois carved and painted cradleboards with **woodland designs** and their **clan** animal.

Iroquois children were taught to respect their parents, elders, and the entire natural world. Adults sometimes told scary tales to teach children how to act properly.

Iroquois children loved to play games. A popular game was called javelin. It was played with a hickory stick and wooden hoop.

An Iroquois cradleboard

CHAPTER 9

Sky Woman

The Iroquois used stories to explain many things about life. The Sky Woman story explained the creation of the earth.

Long ago, Sky Woman fell through the hole in the sky. She entered a world of water and darkness where birds and water animals lived. A flock of geese caught Sky Woman on their wings and placed her on the Great Turtle's back.

The muskrat brought a little bit of mud from the ocean floor to Sky Woman. She placed the mud on the Great Turtle's back. Then Sky Woman began to dance and sing. As she danced, the Great Turtle began to grow. It became what we now call North America.

Today, when there is an earthquake, the Iroquois tell their children that it is just the Great Turtle stretching.

Turtles are sacred in many Native American traditions.

CHAPTER 10

War

The Iroquois were respected for their ability to outwit their enemies. They fought with bows and arrows, knives, and clubs. Arrowheads were made of flint. War clubs were made of stone, wood, or deer antlers. These were also called tomahawks. A tomahawk was used in close combat. It could also be thrown.

Going to war was not taken lightly. Everyone had to agree that the only solution to a problem was to fight. Once everyone agreed to fight, a red tomahawk was hung on a special war post. Black **wampum** was attached to the tomahawk. This meant that the **clans** had agreed to go to war.

The white pine is a symbol of peace. It represents the end of war between the five Iroquois nations, and the formation of the Haudenosaunee.

CHAPTER 11

Contact with Europeans

In 1609, French explorer Samuel de Champlain and his Algonquin guides traveled into Iroquois lands. They fought the Iroquois with guns. The Iroquois had never seen guns before. They could not defend themselves against them.

Eventually, the Iroquois began trading with European explorers and colonists. The Europeans wanted furs from beavers and other animals that the Iroquois trapped. In return, the Iroquois received goods such as metal tools, cooking pots, woven cloth, and guns.

Unfortunately, the Europeans also brought diseases such as measles and smallpox. The Iroquois had never been exposed to these diseases before. So, they had little **immunity**. Many Iroquois people died of these diseases.

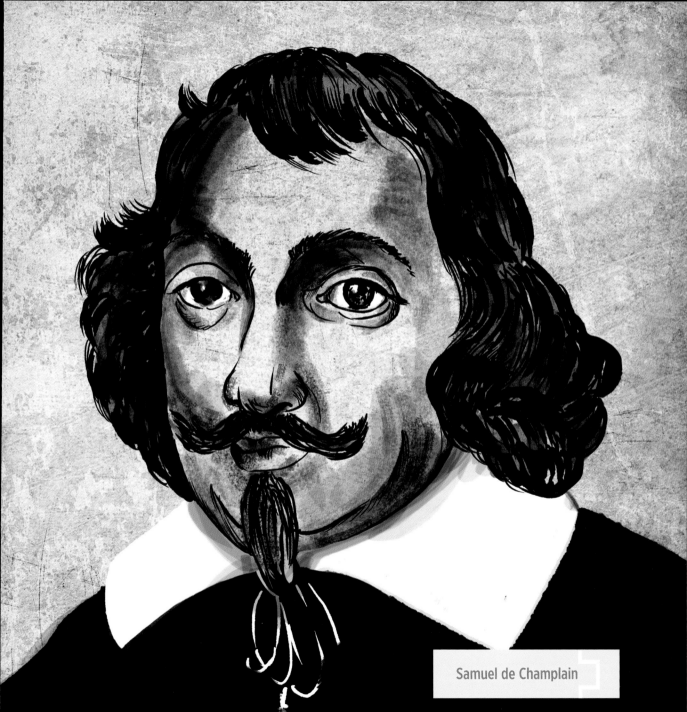

Samuel de Champlain

CHAPTER 12

The Peacemaker

The Peacemaker was a great Huron prophet. He and Onondaga leader Hiawatha (Aiionwatha) began a journey. They wanted to spread the message of peace.

At the time, the Mohawk, Oneida, Onondaga, Cayuga, and Seneca were at war with each other. When the Peacemaker reached the Mohawks, he told them that he came with a message of peace. The Mohawks wanted him to prove it.

The Peacemaker said he would climb into a tree near the river where there were dangerous rapids. Then the Mohawks should cut the tree down so he would fall into the river. But he said he would return.

The Mohawks followed his instructions. The Peacemaker fell into the rapids. The next morning, the Mohawks found the Peacemaker sitting by their fire, as he had promised. They listened to his message and accepted the **Great Law of Peace**.

Today, the rapids that swept the Peacemaker away are called Cohoes Falls.

CHAPTER 13

The Iroquois Today

Today, there are more than 125,000 Iroquois living in North America. Most live in Ontario and Quebec in Canada, and in New York, Wisconsin, and Oklahoma in the United States.

Most Iroquois no longer live in longhouses, but they use them for ceremonies. And many Iroquois people follow the traditional ways. This includes taking care of the **environment** and preserving Iroquois **culture**.

Today, Iroquois people hold many types of jobs. Many Iroquois have become doctors, lawyers, and teachers. Many Iroquois men are known for doing steelwork on high-rise structures. But there are still chiefs, **clan** mothers, and faithkeepers. It is their duty to protect the traditional ways for future generations.

Iroquois dancers celebrate and share their culture at the Crawford Lake Iroquoian Village in Ontario, Canada.

Glossary

alliance—a union of nations formed by agreement for some special purpose.

breechcloth—a piece of cloth, usually worn by men. It wraps between the legs and around the waist.

clan—an extended family sharing a common ancestor.

confederacy—a union of peoples joined together for a specific purpose.

cradleboard—a decorative flat board with a wooden band at the top that protects the baby's head.

culture—the customs, arts, and tools of a nation or people at a certain time.

environment—nature and everything in it, such as the land, sea, and air.

Great Law of Peace—a set of principles that teach how people should live in peace and harmony with each other and with the Natural World. It makes sure that the Natural World and the traditional teachings are preserved for future generations.

immunity—the ability to resist a disease.

Indigenous—people native to a certain place.

quill—a large, stiff feather or a sharp spine.

rafter—a slanting beam of a roof.

smoke hole—an opening in the roof of a longhouse to allow smoke to go out.

wampum—cylinder-shaped beads made from clam and snail shells. Wampum was woven into belts and strung on strings. It was used for ceremony, and as a form of barter and trade.

woodland design—a design made of symbols representing vines, leaves, and flowers.

ONLINE RESOURCES

Booklinks
NONFICTION NETWORK
FREE! ONLINE NONFICTION RESOURCES

To learn more about the Iroquois, please visit **abdobooklinks.com** or scan this QR code. These links are routinely monitored and updated to provide the most current information available.

Index